PRECIPITATION, DESOLATION
AND
SALVATION

Precipitation, Desolation and Salvation
by James FitzGerald
Published by
www.jamfitz.com

For permissions contact: requests@jamfitz.com

Cover Design by James FitzGerald.

ISBN: 979-8-9871831-0-6
Library of Congress Control Number: 2022948804
Printed in USA
1st Edition

Dedicated to the people I have forgotten.

PRECIPITATING FASCINATION

Precipitation fascinating,

Abdul turned to face the sky

And felt the cool rain falling gently

As it had for ten days now.

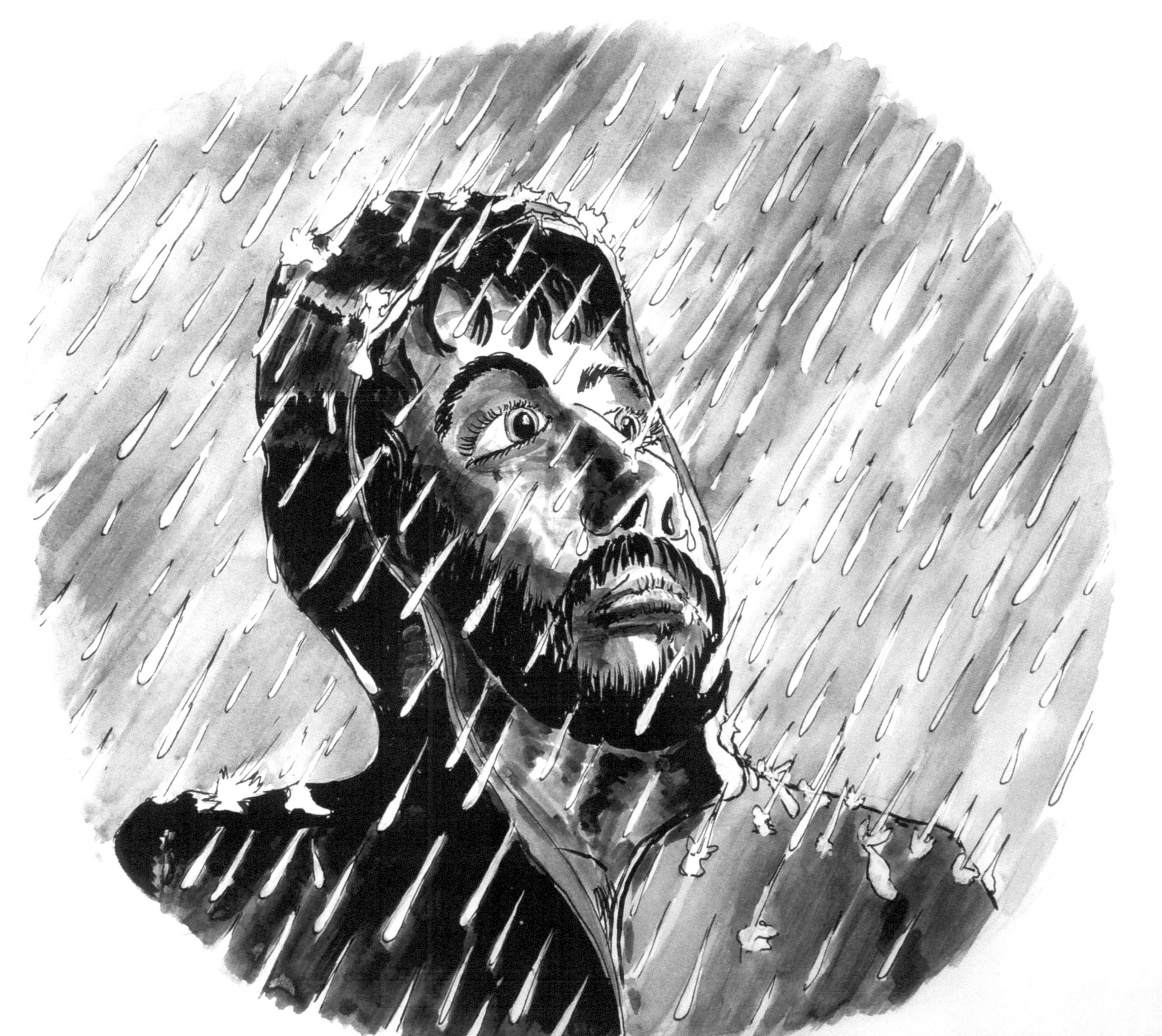

Shamir turned, his face all wet,

And said, "It seems this storm shall never stop.

Perhaps the old fool was correct,

The mountains might not be safe now!"

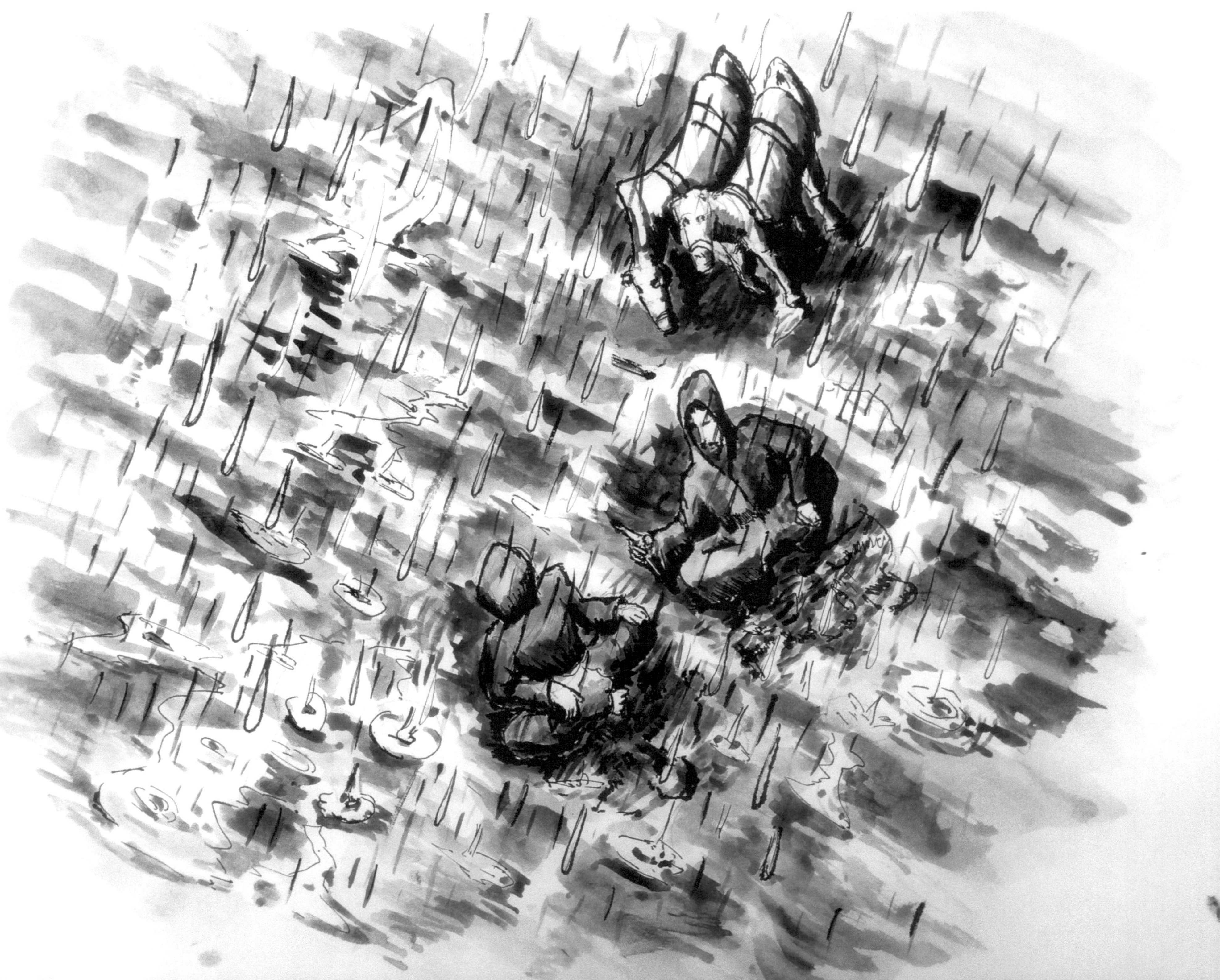

"You camel jockey," Abdul replied.

"You're even more insane than he!

This fertile valley has surely seen

Yaweh's tears fall hard before."

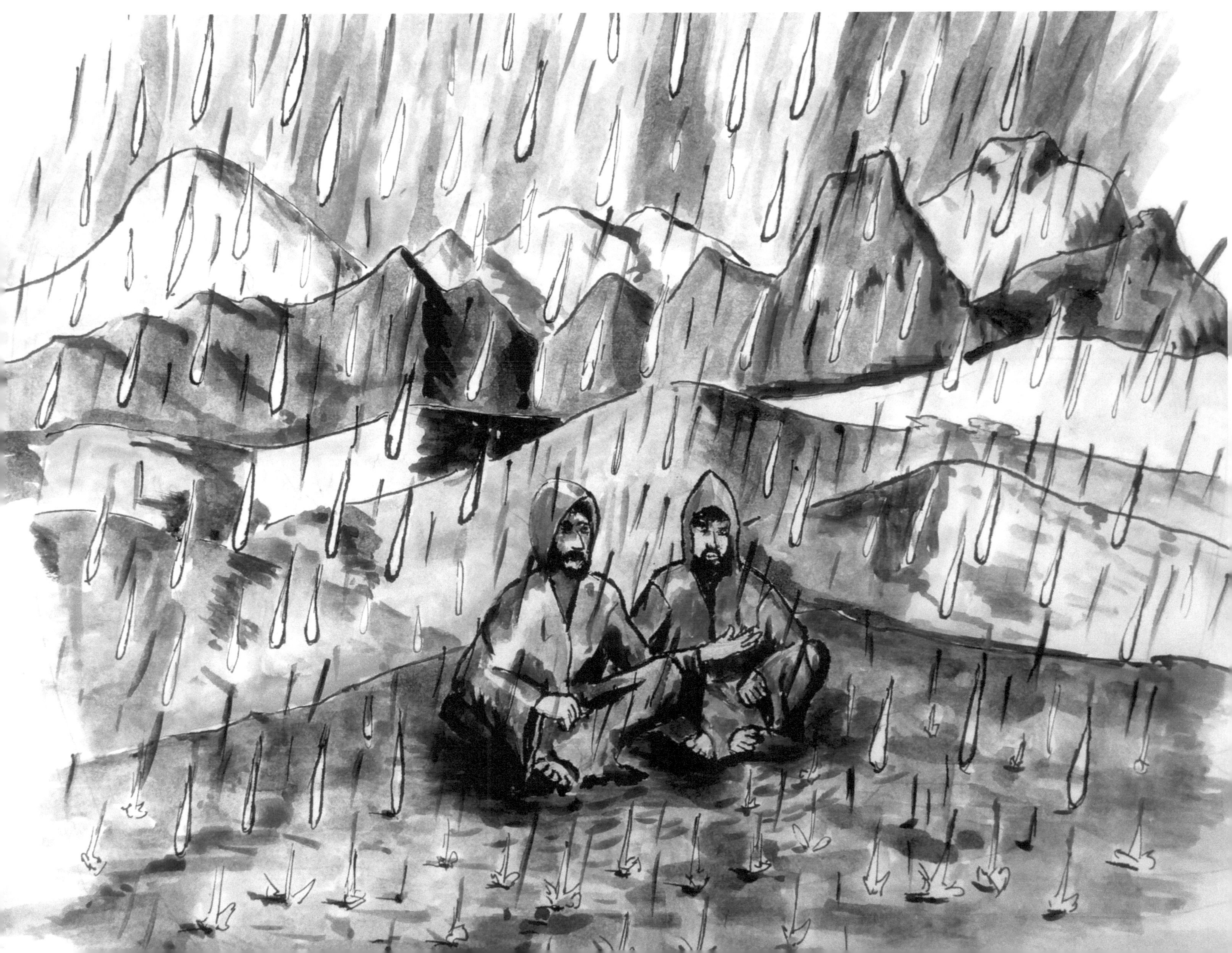

Precipitating fascination,

A ewe bellowed and was downward swept

From what was left of the pasture

Into the murky waters.

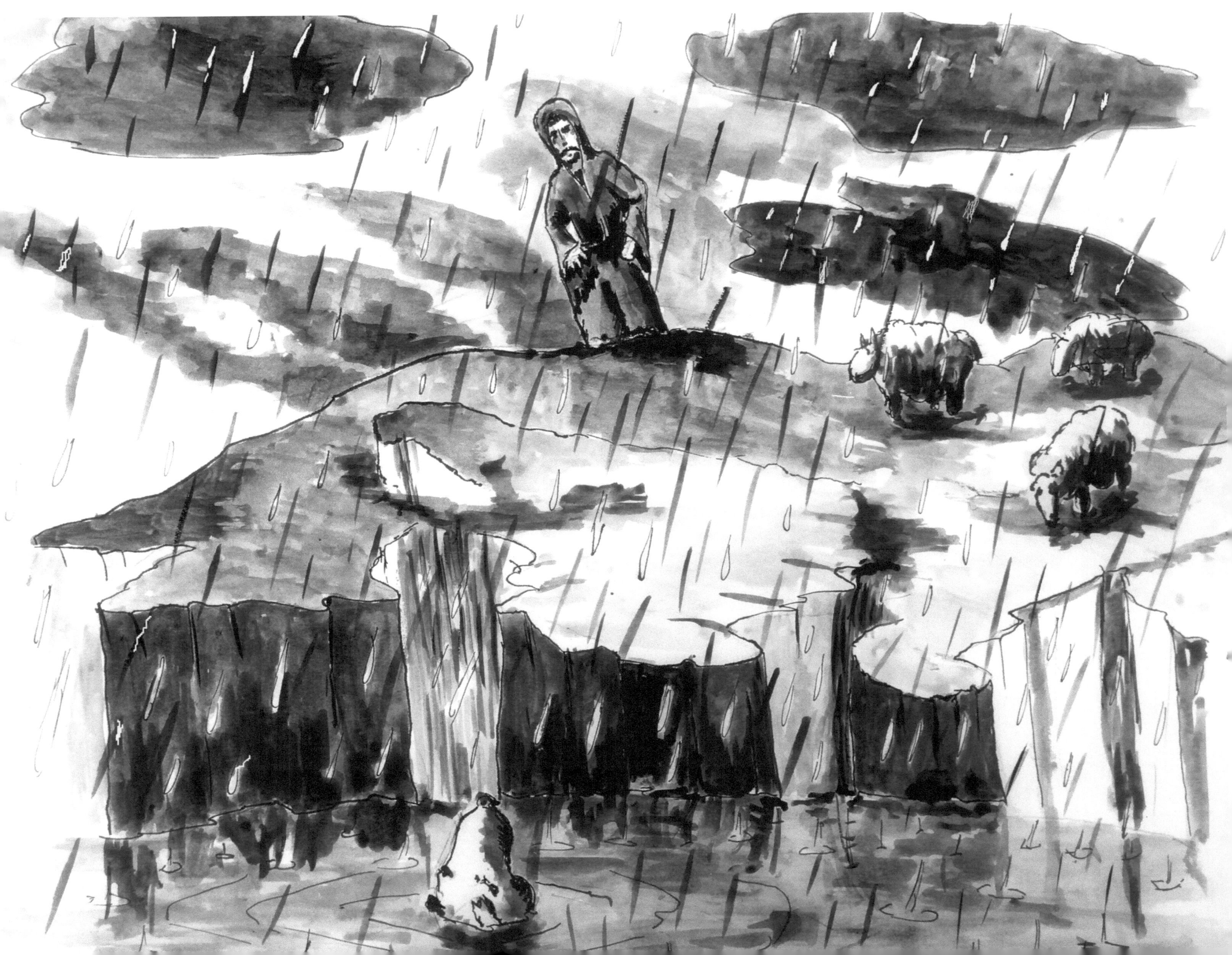

"Third sheep that I have lost this morning,"
Shamir said in an off-hand way.

"A curse upon his generations!"
Abdul chuckled at this line.

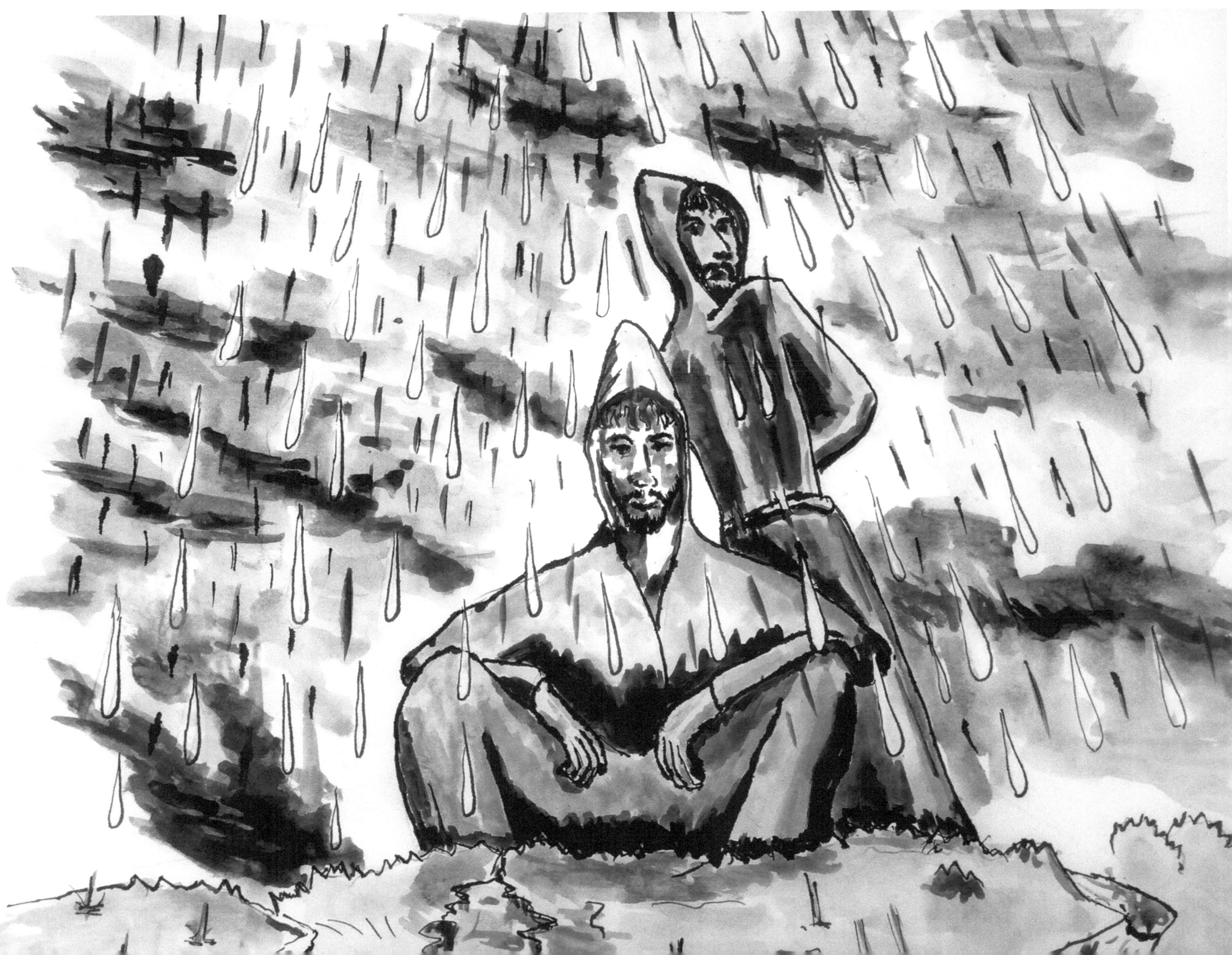

"The river is rising steadily now,

Abdul, you know, I am getting scared!"

But Abdul was lost, laughing endless,

At the cold rain and at the sky.

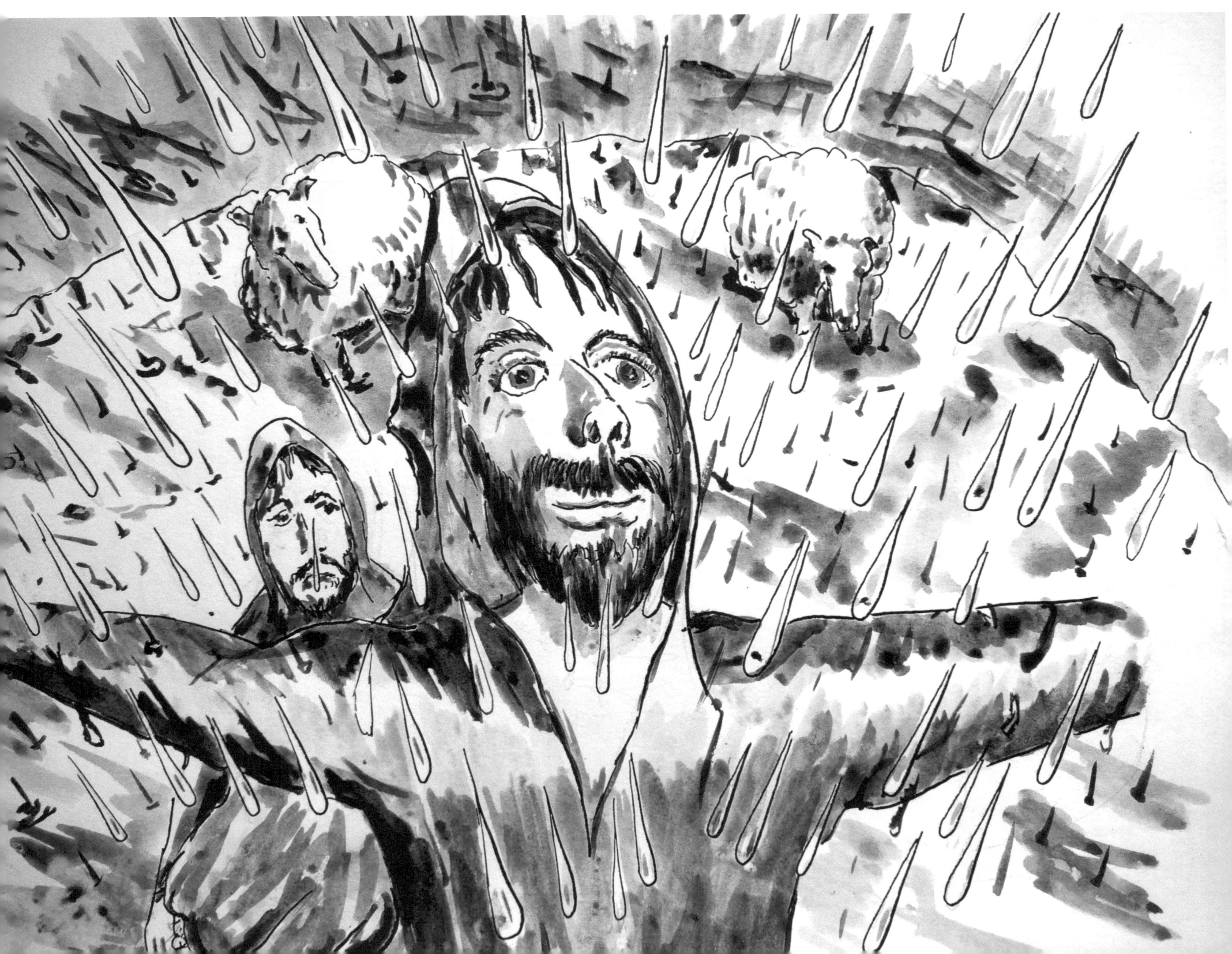

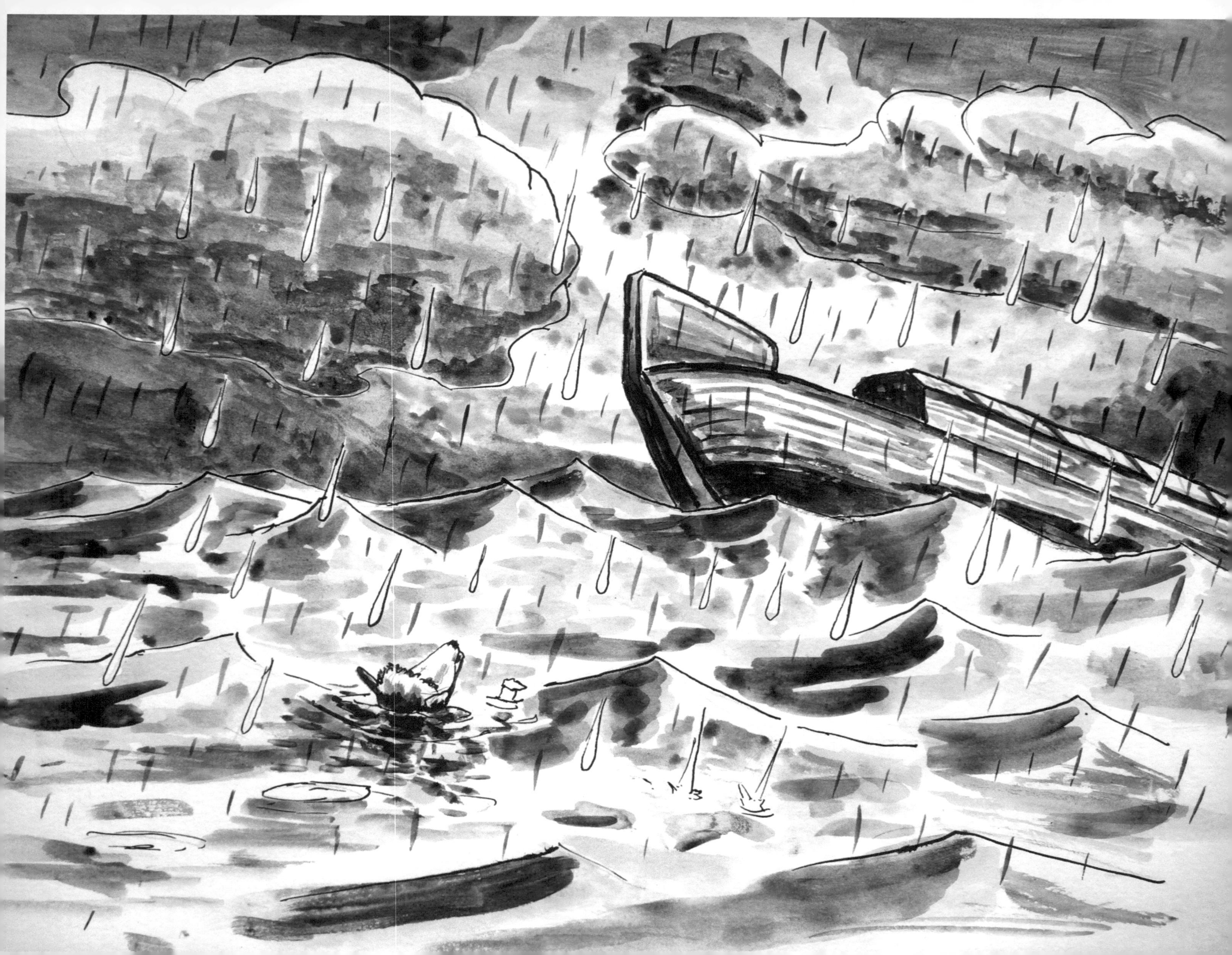

A SAD LOT

I met a man on the road from Zoar.

He had two women with him,

Both very young.

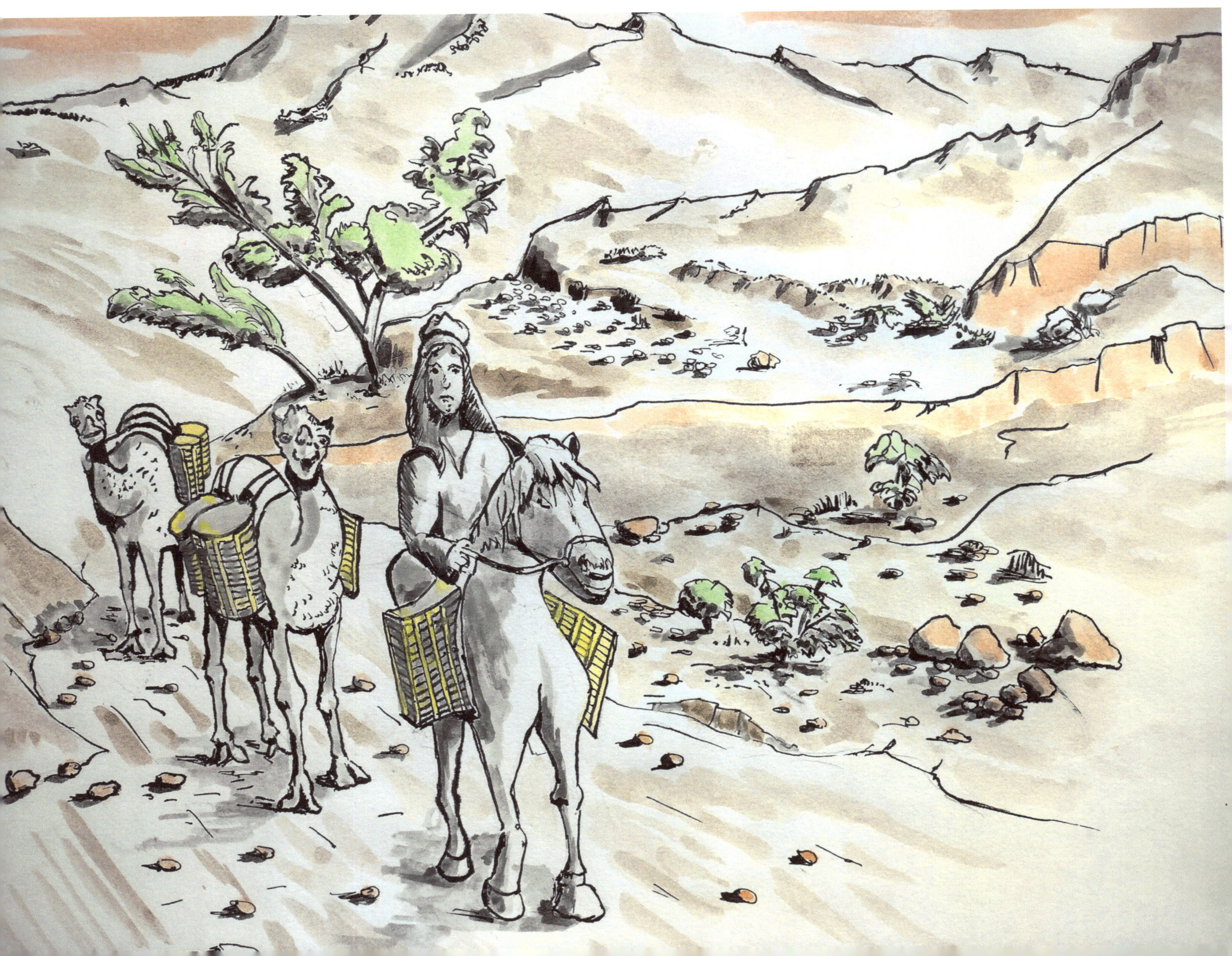

The pain on his face concealed his age

The same way the haze in the sky concealed the sun.

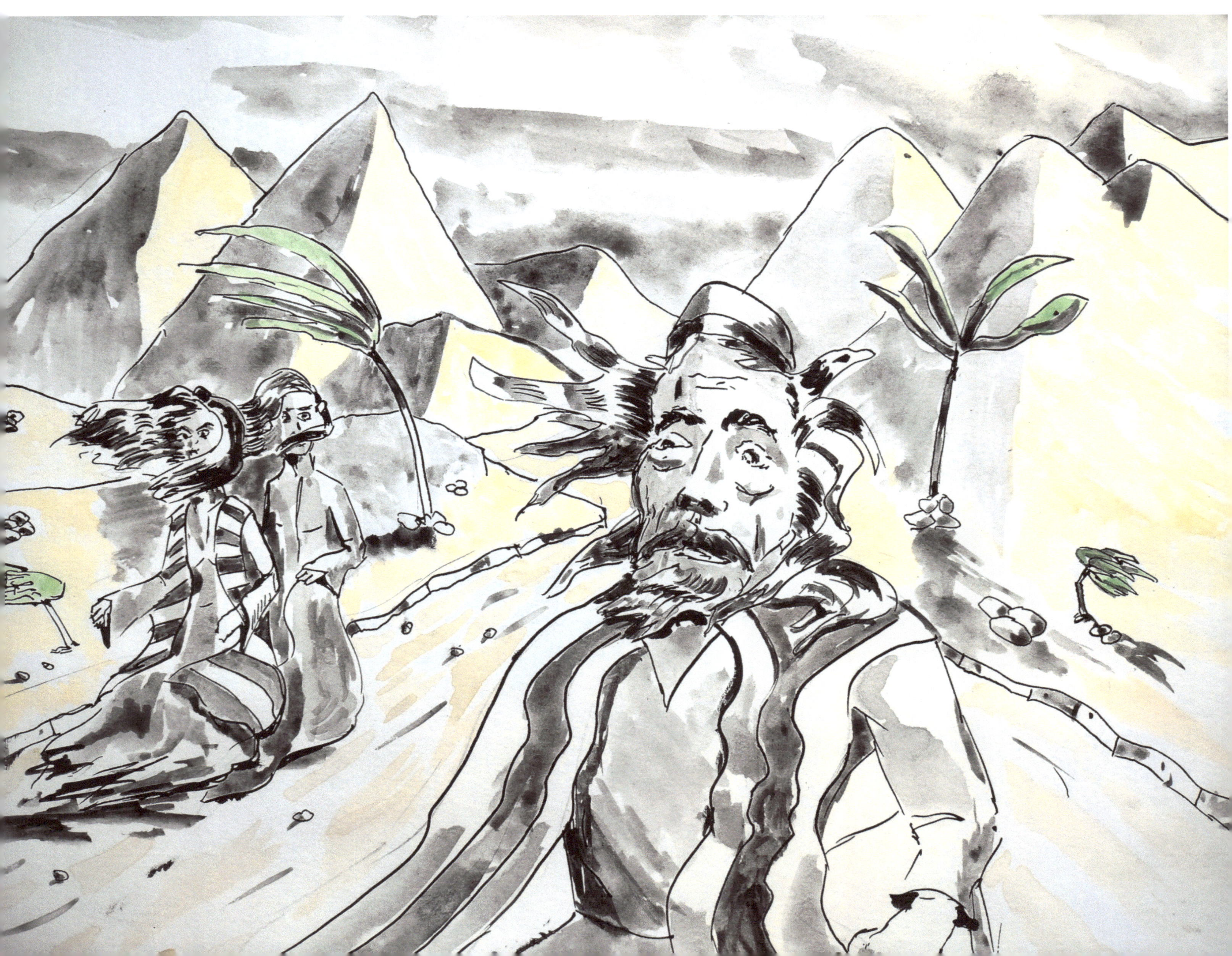

I started to ask, in a hestiant voice,

"Are you lost, can I help you somehow?"

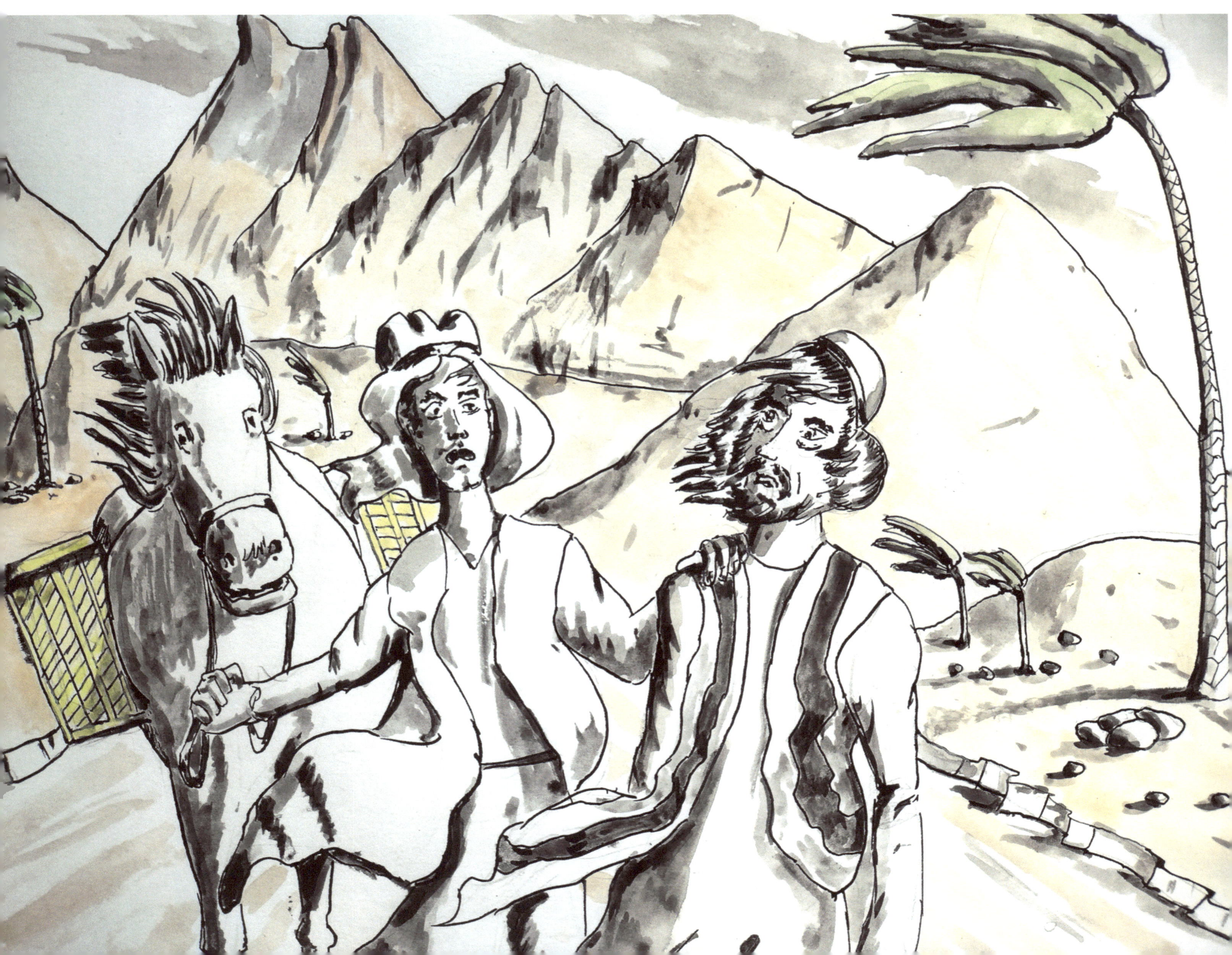

When his sigh struck me deeply,

Like the last drop of a storm,

Or the last wave of high tide,

Something final that no question could change.

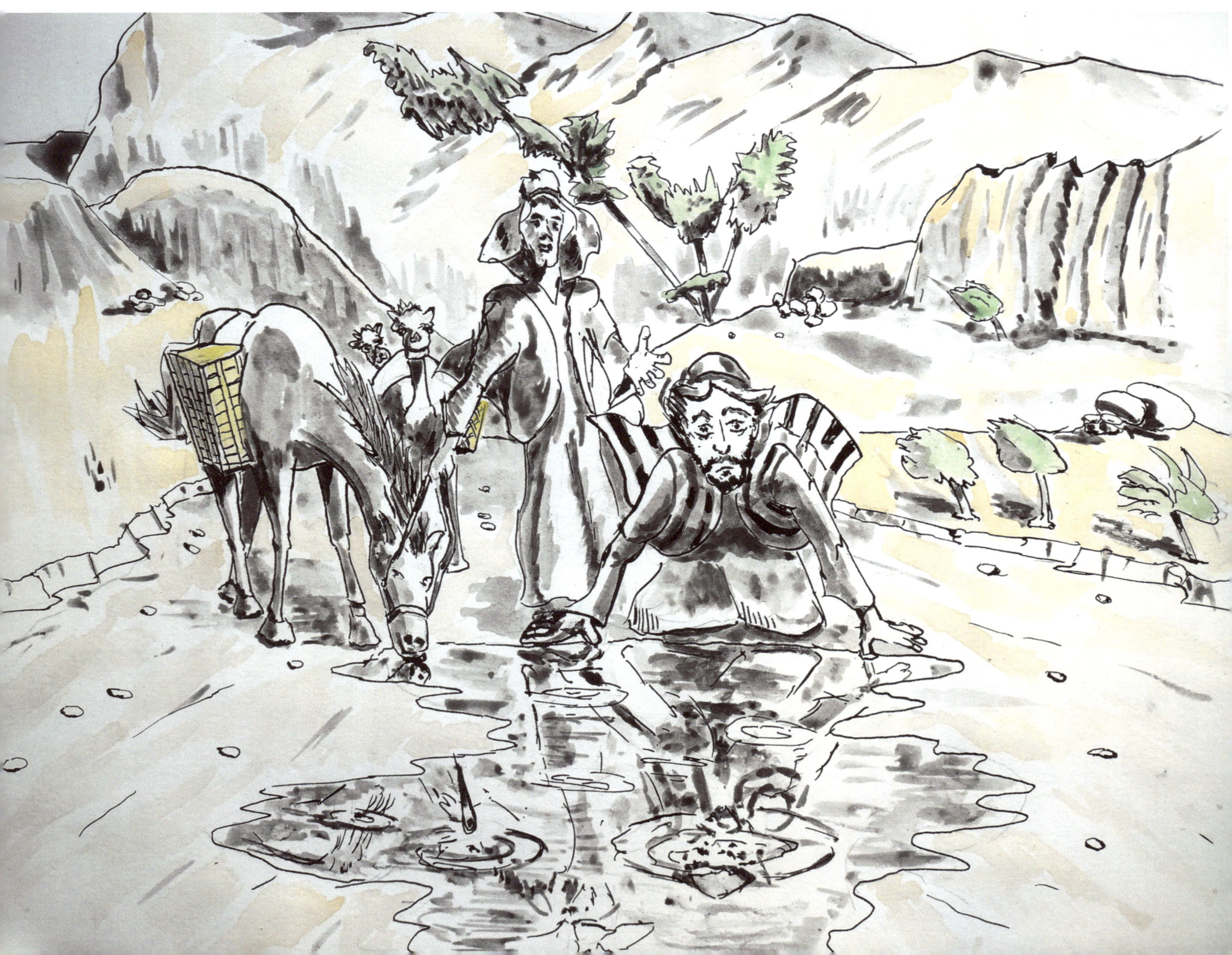

"Judgements," he whispered.

And then he said nothing more,

But continued to stare at the familiar dead rocks

That line the road as you go from Zoar.

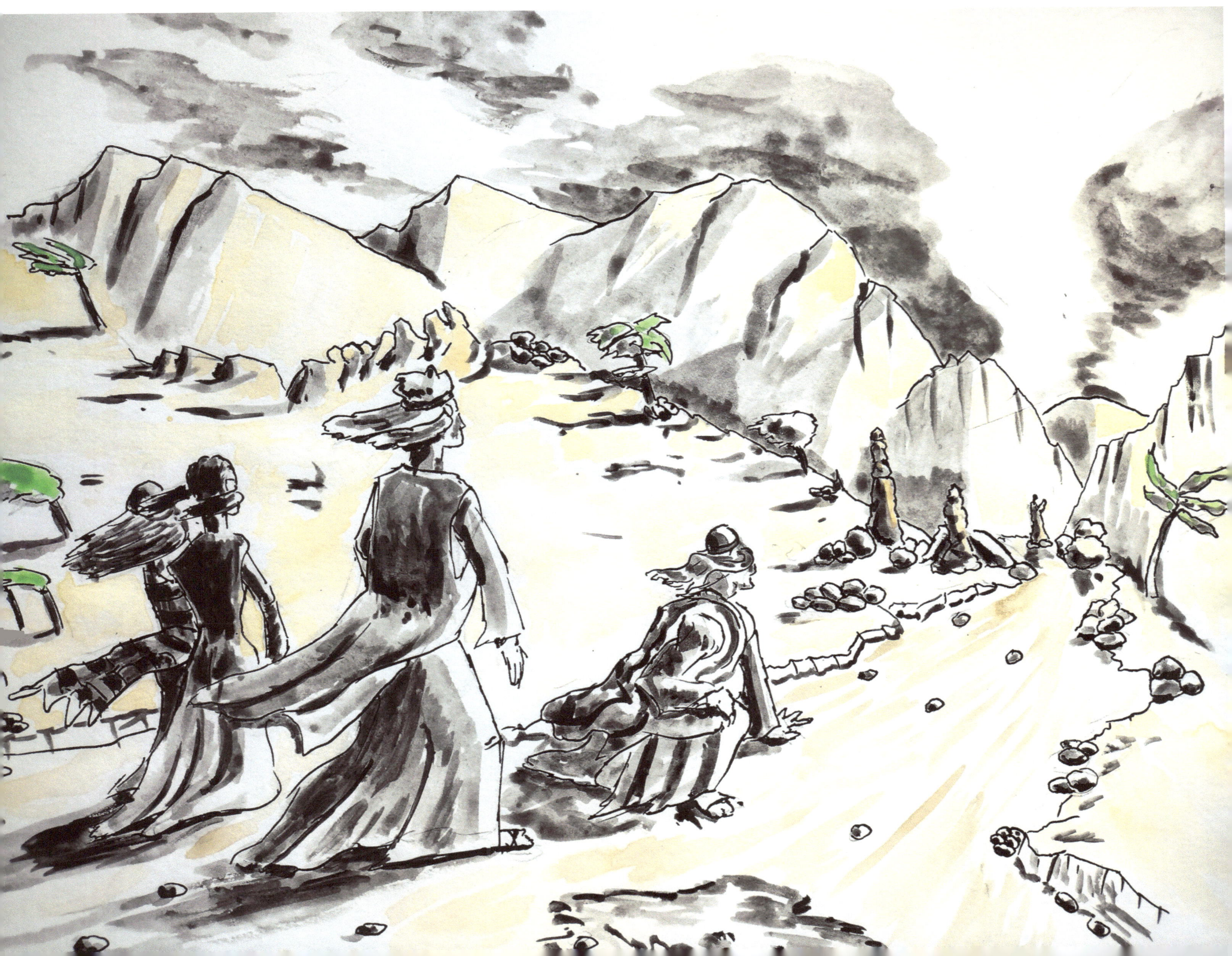

"Judgements!" he said louder.

"Everyone is forewarned!"

And I departed for a city,

That I found later was gone.

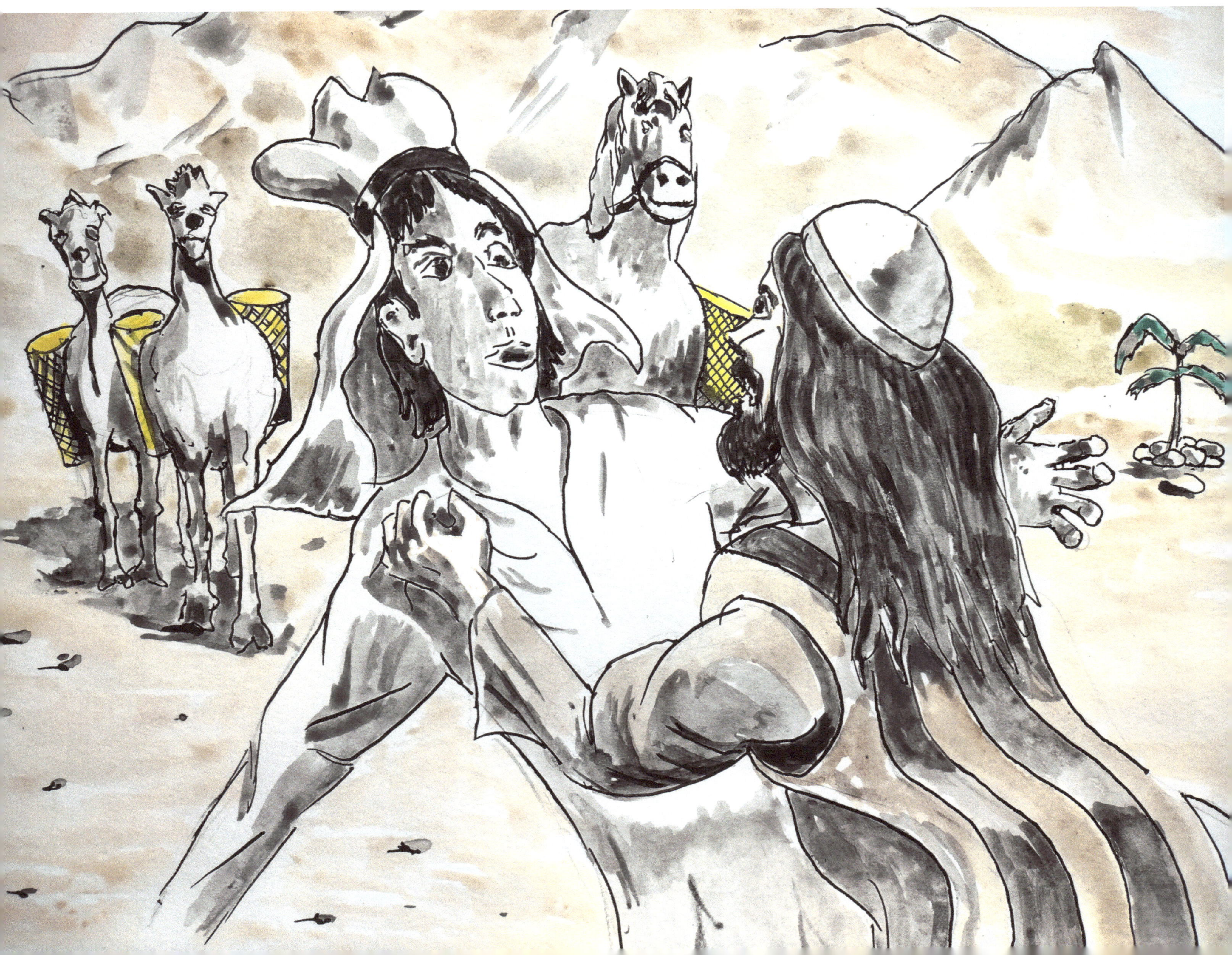

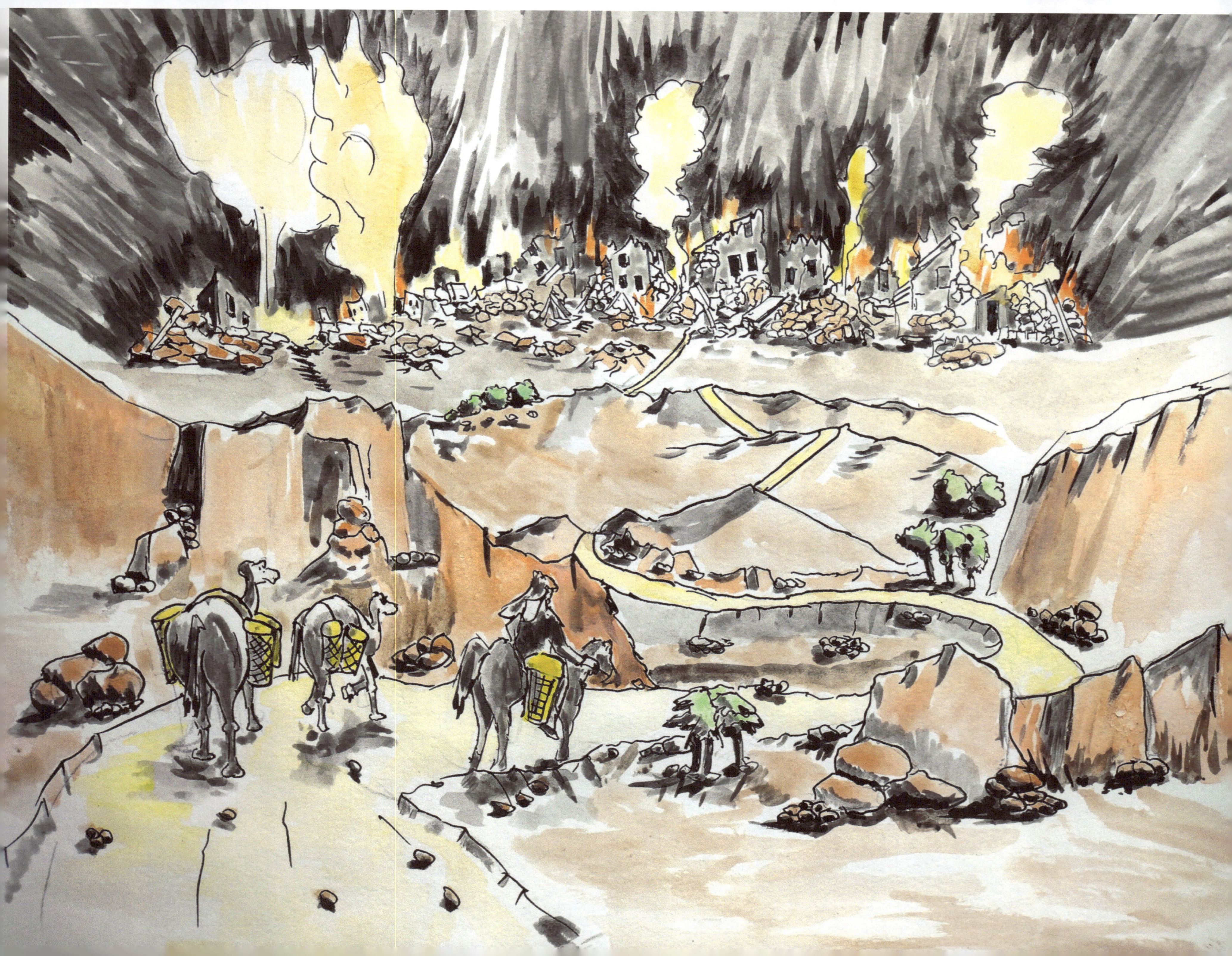

JOHN'S LAMENT

The glass of wine you drank from,

Set on the long table half emptied,

As if you left suddenly

In fear of your own friends.

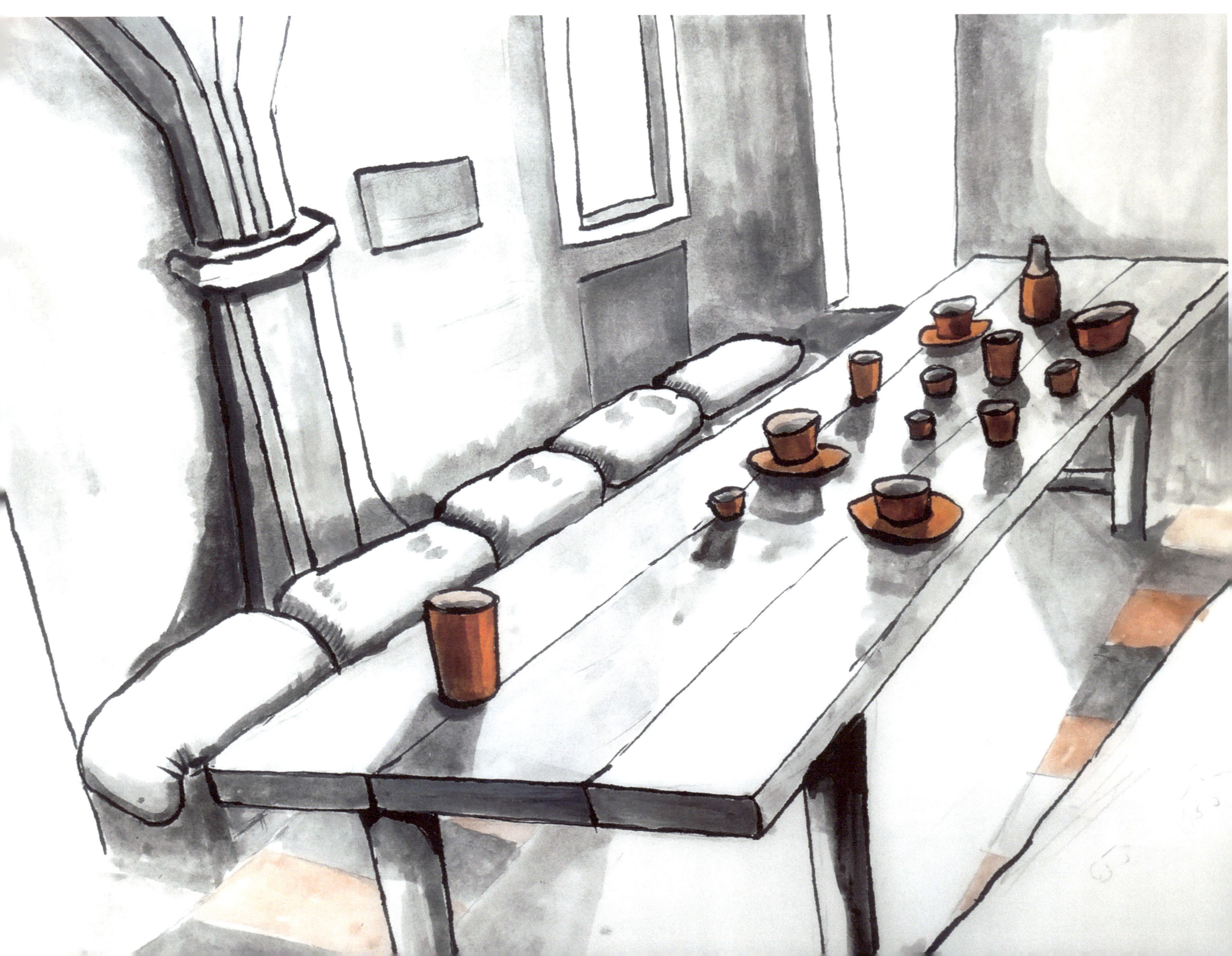

The party died painfully,

You were one of the first to go.

Uncertainty betrayed you,

They all mentioned it behind your back.

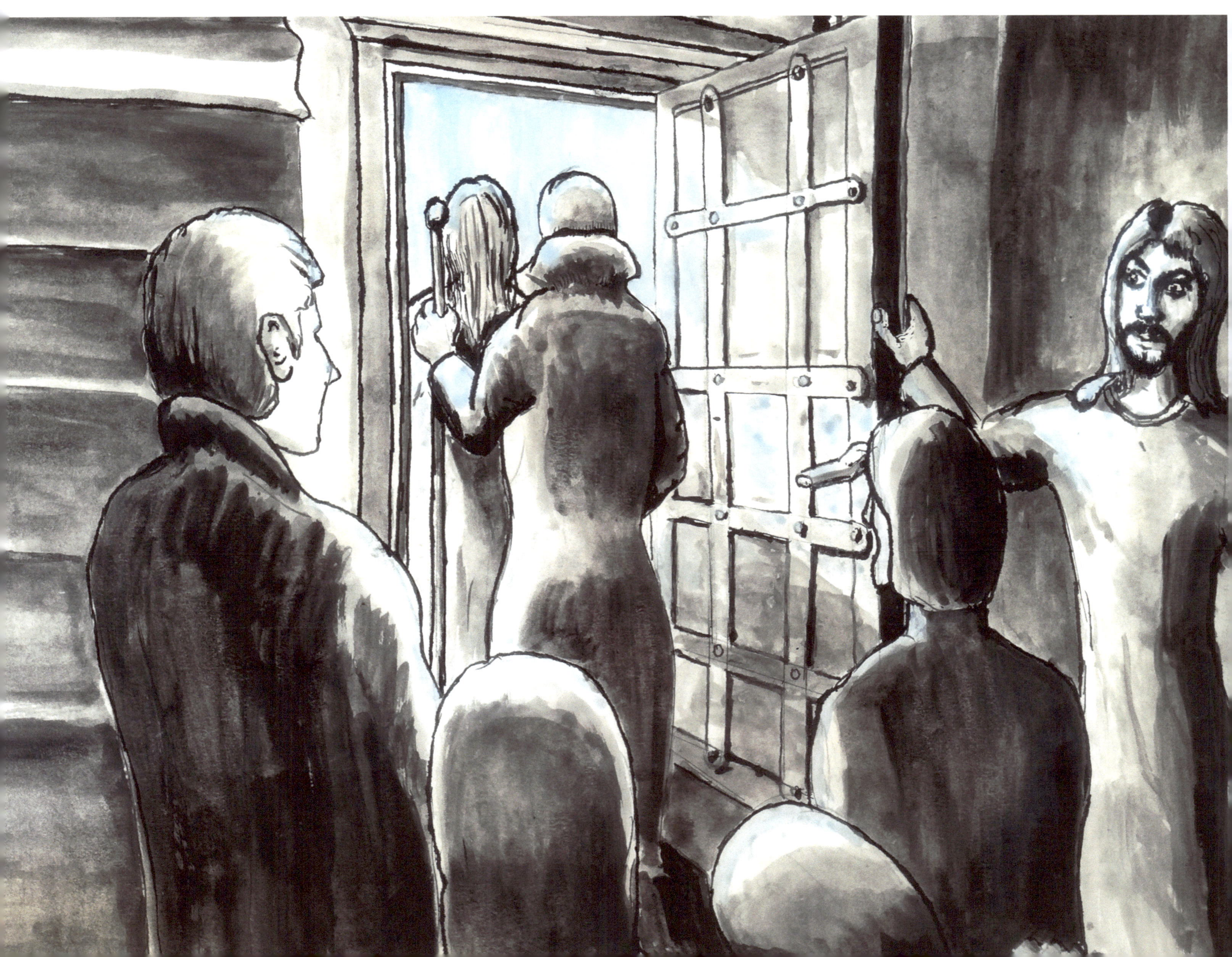

The empty dusk time shadows

Gravely hear your strange soliloquy.

Your spoken word yet echoes

On the cold floors and the hallway walls.

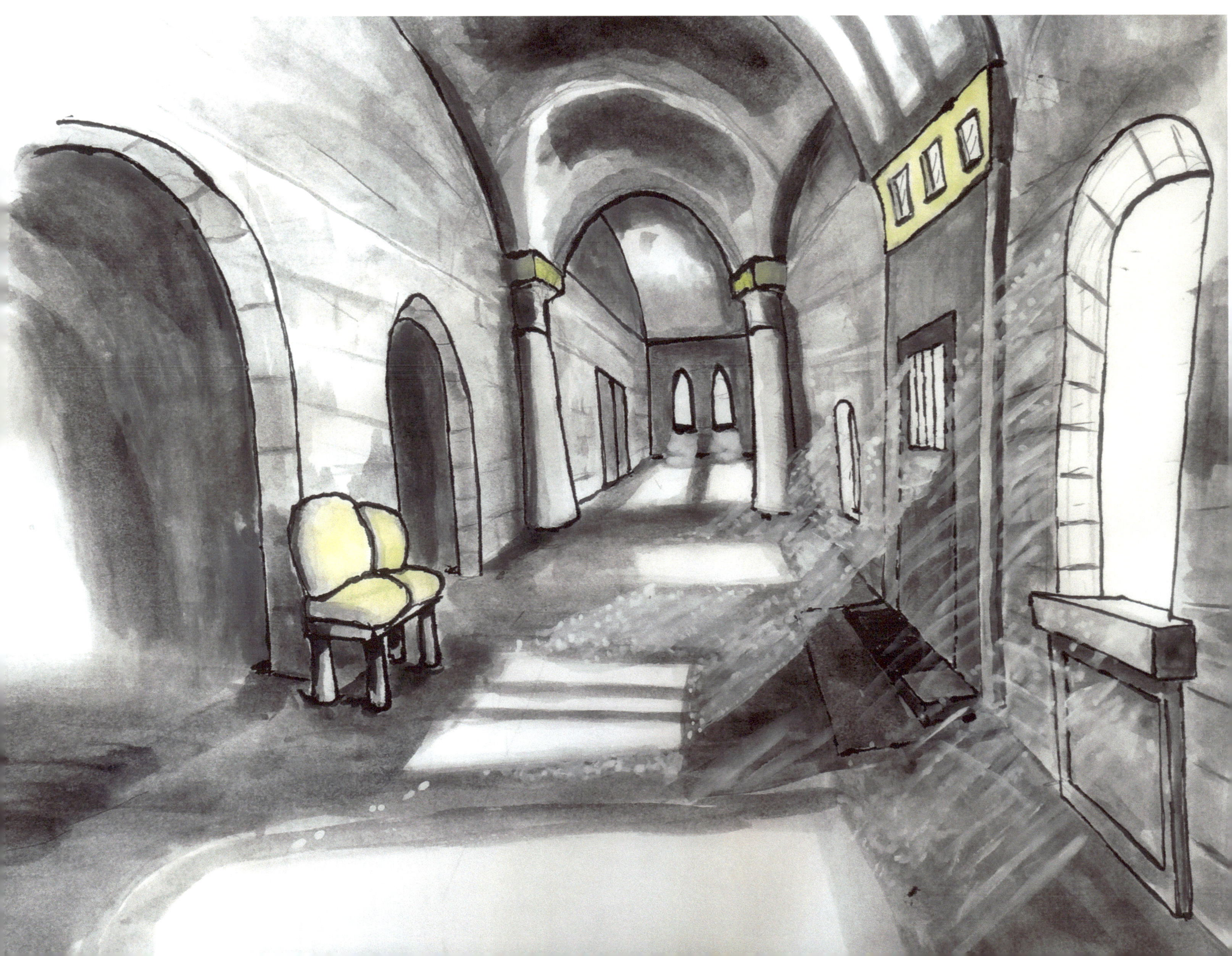

They say that you walked in the garden

And that you seemed quite apart from yourself.

Not understanding your motives,

I felt lost and alone.

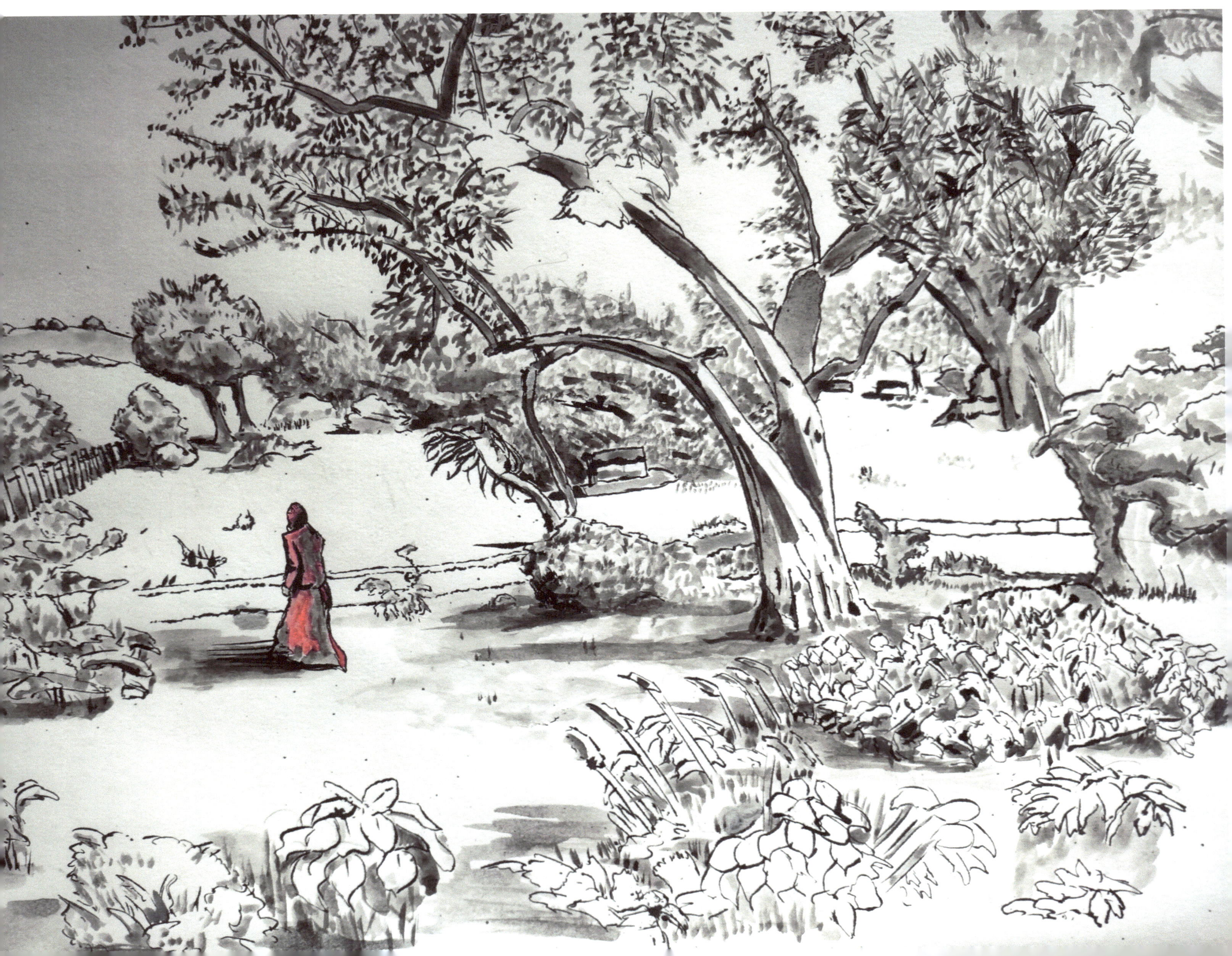

Couldn't you have told me the problems

That made you so remote from me?

Perhaps I could have dispelled them

With a joke or a laugh or a song.

But no, something about you made you truly alone.

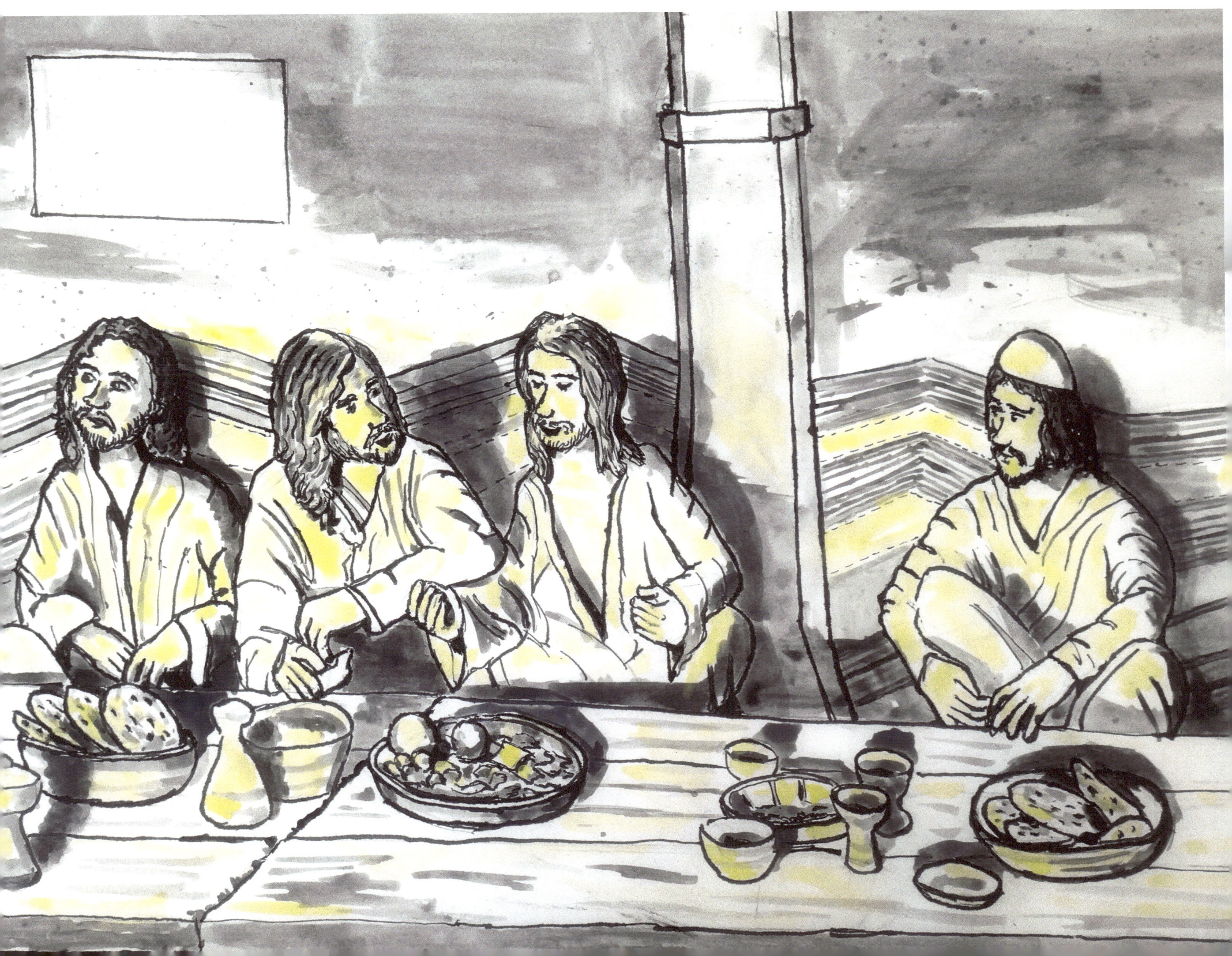

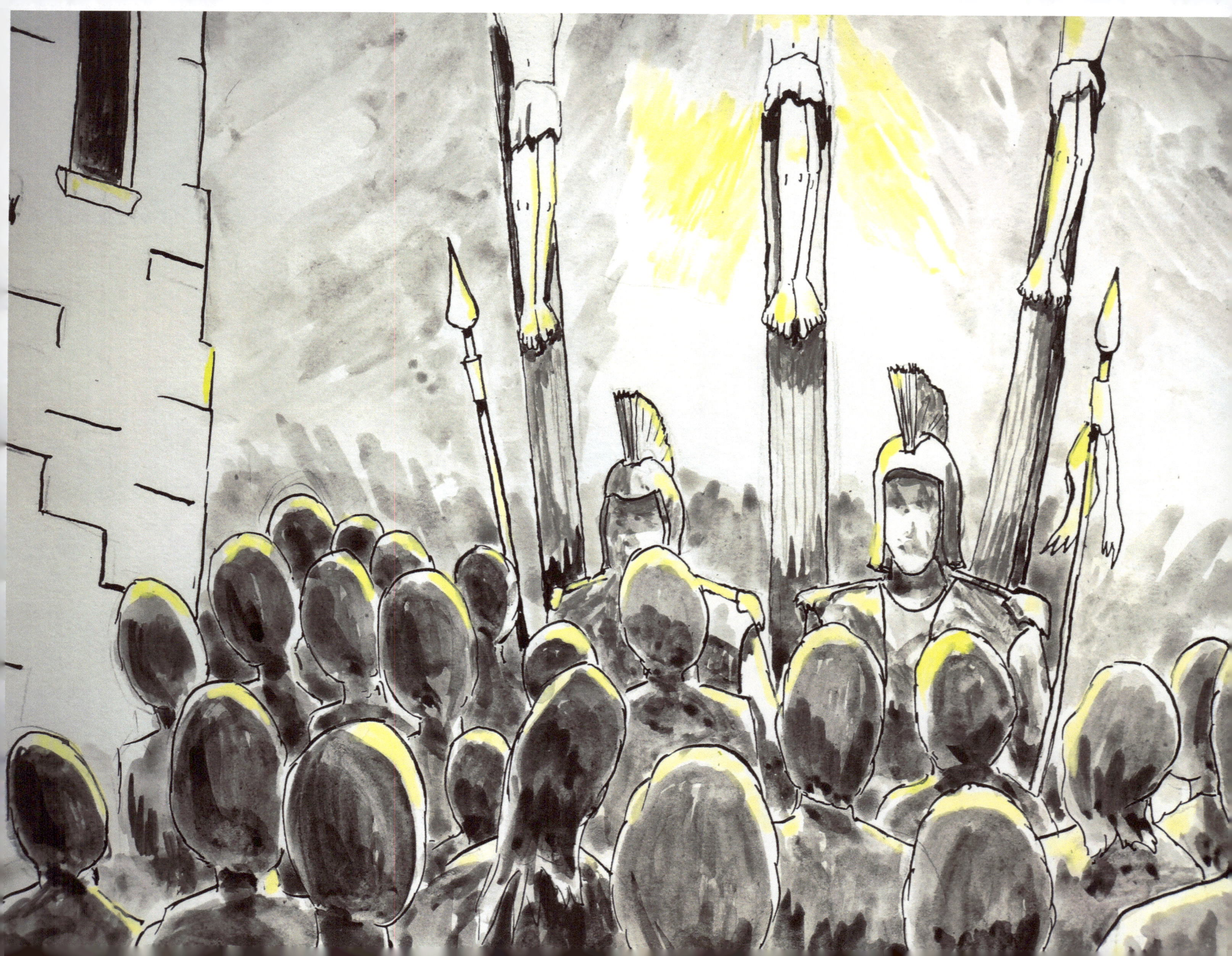

About the Author

James FitzGerald is a graduate of the University of Cincinnati.

A long time computer industry consultant, involved in many projects for major corporations.

He now avoids logic, mangement and overtime.

www.ingramcontent.com/pod-product-compliance
Lightning Source LLC
Chambersburg PA
CBHW042132150726
48005CB00028B/789